W9-BRG-535

Also by Evelyn McFarlane & James Saywell

If . . . (Questions for the Game of Life)

If² . . . (500 New Questions for the Game of Life)

If³ . . . (Questions for the Game of Love)

If . . . Questions for the Soul

How Far Will You Go?

If . . . Questions for Parents

Would You?

Evelyn McFarlane
&
James Saywell

Would You?

Questions
to Challenge
Your Beliefs

VILLARD  NEW YORK

Copyright © 2000 by Evelyn McFarlane and James Saywell

All rights reserved under International and Pan-American Copyright
Conventions. Published in the United States by Villard Books, a division of
Random House, Inc., New York, and simultaneously in Canada by Random
House of Canada Limited, Toronto.

VILLARD BOOKS and colophon are registered trademarks of Random House, Inc.

Library of Congress Cataloging-in-Publication Data is available.

ISBN: 0-375-50243-2

Villard Books website address: www.villard.com

Printed in the United States of America on acid-free paper

4 6 8 9 7 5 3

First Edition

BOOK DESIGN BY BARBARA MARKS

Introduction

We want to know:

> What's important to you?
> What do you believe?
> How strongly do you believe it?

Most of the questions in this book you will never have to answer. (Unless your life is *very* interesting.) But how would you answer them if you had to? Could you answer them at all? Are you sure what you would do if you had an extremely difficult, or extremely tempting, decision to make? After all, our beliefs—what we stand for, or would fight for—define us, from the kind of person our parents raised to the kind of child we have brought up. And, of course, the type of society we contribute to.

Would you kill to save your child? Someone else's child? Your parent? Would you commit perjury to shield a lover? Would you sacrifice one of your senses to end world hunger? Would you give up sex for money? Give up money for love? Love for immortality?

Even if your own life never demands the answers to questions like these, that doesn't mean you shouldn't have to answer them . . . if you can.

Sometimes what we think we would do in a hypothetical situation isn't what we end up doing in real life. Or, what we think other people should do turns out not to be what we do ourselves. Are we hypocritical, or just confused? Do we have double standards? Are these moving ethical targets? How do we explain our actions to the mirror, or to our kids? It matters. Know yourself.

Aside: We suggest you answer the first question of each pair before reading the second.

Would You?

Prefer fame
or respect?

Would you . . .

Say you are prouder of your
accomplishments or of your character?

Prefer infamy or anonymity?

Would you...

Prefer to be recognized in your
lifetime or by posterity?

Would you . . .

Rather have
more brains,
more beauty,
or more
chutzpah?

Rather relinquish some of your brains, some
of your beauty, or some of your chutzpah?

Would you ...

Give the police more power in exchange for a lower crime rate?

Sacrifice civil liberties for personal economic gain?

Rather have prevented slavery, the Vietnam War, the nuclear attack on Japan, or the experience of Native American peoples?

Would you ...

Pay reparations to any of the victims of those catastrophes?

Cheat on an exam?

Would you . . .

Write your child's
college entrance essay?

Would you ...

Rather plot revenge on your boss, a colleague, a relative, or your ex?

Prefer to live in a society that places more value on justice or on forgiveness?

Would you ...

Prefer a
society of
science but
no art, or
of art but
no science?

Advise your child
to study art or to
study science?

10

Be more afraid to
tell your parents that
you were gay or that
you had committed
a serious crime?

Would you . . .

Be more afraid to hear that your child was gay
or that they had committed a serious crime?

Take a pay cut to end homelessness
in your country?

Would you...

Take a pay cut to end
homelessness in another
country?

Would you . . .

Interfere with a rival's
promotion?

Interfere with an ex's
love life?

Would you . . .

Clone your own body
as a source of organs for
future transplants?

Clone your child if they
experienced an early,
tragic death?

Illegally buy a human organ
to save your child's life?

Would you . . .

Donate your eyes to
give your child sight?

Place more value on the
praise of your parents or
of your children?

Would you . . .

Be more likely to disappoint your
children or your parents?

Would you ...

Prefer to be a better athlete, businessperson, cook, lover, or moralist?

Rather date a jock, CEO, chef, sex therapist, or minister?

Would you . . .

Consider promiscuity
a character weakness?

Like more sex?

Value chastity more in
a man or in a woman?

Would you
. . .

Judge a person's sex life differently
if they're twenty rather than forty?

Would you...

Try to dissuade your young teenager from having sex if the risk of disease and pregnancy were eliminated?

Accept your son being sexually active at a younger age than your daughter?

Keep all
pornography
away
from your
teenagers?

Would you ...

Encourage your mate to use
pornography as an aphrodisiac?

Would you ...

Be able to forgive your child
anything at all?

Be able to forgive your mate
anything at all?

Choose a career for your child,
given the possibility?

Would you . . .

Ever refuse to attend your child's wedding
to protest their choice of partner?

Send your child to an
expensive school if you knew
that they would become a
truck driver anyway?

Would you . . .

Rather live in a society in which everyone
gets the same education or one in which
select people receive a great one?

Would you . . .

Consider any
sacrifice too great
for the sake of your
children?

Go to prison in place
of your child?

Would you . . .

Rather be a
good spouse or
a good parent?

Marry someone knowing they
would be a bad parent to your kids?

Consider yourself a
good citizen?

Would you

. . .

Fight for your country in an unjust war?

Move to another country that you considered morally superior?

Would you...

Move to another country for an easier life?

Would you . . .

Turn down a great job offer from a company with questionable ethics?

Accept a Christmas bonus knowing the money was "dirty"?

Would you . . .

Say you are capable of
white-collar crime?

Steal a pen from the office
supply closet or make a
personal long-distance call at
the company's expense?

Prefer a stormy relationship with your parents or an indifferent one?

Would you...

Rather your child made you proud or showed you great affection?

Say that happiness
is found or made?

Would you . . .

Say that the more
power you have
to control life, the
richer it is?

Would you . . .

Like to know more
about your mate?

Choose to know
everything about
your mate?

Would you . . .

Rather be a
great lover
or have one?

Say that you have a
responsibility, in a romantic
relationship, to fulfill your
partner's sexual needs?

Rather marry for
passion or for
compatibility?

End a relationship
when the physical
passion stops?

Say that passion is necessary
in everyone's life?

Say that passion or ambition
will carry you farther in life?

Be more likely to follow your heart or your head?

Would you . . .

Give more importance to what you know or what you believe?

Would you ...

Be more fearful
of what you
don't know or
what you do?

Say fears have more helped
you or more hurt you?

Expect your character to be greatly different if you were a member of the opposite sex?

Would you . . .

Ever want to date yourself as a member of the opposite sex?

Undergo open-heart
surgery if it was
to be performed by
a female doctor?

Would you . . .

Choose a male or a female lawyer to represent
you if you were accused of murder?

Would you . . .

Willingly fight
side by side
with a woman
in combat?

Encourage your daughter to enter
a field normally reserved for men?

41

Would you . . .

Be uncomfortable
earning less than
your spouse?

Be upset if your son
gave up his career
to become a
househusband?

Rather age well
physically or mentally?

Would you . . .

Support any and all medical procedures
that extend a patient's life?

Support genetic research designed to slow
the human aging process?

Would you...

Say that death is the
worst thing that can
happen to you?

Would you ...

Consider
culture to be
advancing
or declining?

Rather see a blockbuster movie
or a documentary?

Would you ...

Prefer to compose an extraordinary piece of music, write a great novel, direct an amazing film, or design a beautiful building?

Say culture has received a greater contribution from the written word or from the visual image?

Break a law that you
considered unjust?

Would you . . .

Turn in your parent upon discovering
they were a war criminal in hiding?

Pierce an intimate
body part to make your
lover happy?

Would you . . .

Allow your child to pierce any part
of their body they wanted?

Would you ...

Surgically improve your body at the request of your lover?

Be disturbed to learn that part of your lover's body was fake?

Would you . . .

Get out of the car of someone who was driving unsafely?

Vote for a law that held passengers as well as drivers responsible for drunk driving?

Feel uncomfortable
to be asked, at a
dinner party, how
much you earn?

Would you . . .

Share your specific
financial situation with
your children?

Insist on knowing how much
your betrothed was worth?

Would you...

Automatically divide
your assets with your
spouse upon marriage?

Would you . . .

Help a
stranger
who was
being
mugged?

Carry a gun while
walking through
a dangerous
neighborhood
late at night?

Would you . . .

Feel less guilty about stealing from a big company than from a small one?

Be more inclined to sue someone because they were insured or wealthy?

Desire total freedom?

Would you . . .

Claim that a billionaire
has more freedom or that
a pauper does?

Rather vote for
someone smarter
than you or just
like you in a
presidential
election?

Hire someone who was
better-looking than you?

Would you ...

Be more upset to discover that your mother was having an affair or that your father was?

More readily disapprove of a man dating a much younger cookie, or a woman dating a much younger stud?

Would you ...

Prefer to be thought naturally talented or to be considered hardworking?

Resent having your success attributed to luck?

Sooner lend someone
your hairbrush,
toothbrush, or
swimsuit?

Would you . . .

Feel more uncomfortable if a stranger touched
you on your cheek, your bottom, or your feet?

Consider yourself more practical or more frivolous?

Would you...

Rather have a free shopping day at Home Depot or at Saks?

Say that
your life
so far has
been easy or
difficult?

Would you . . .

Say that you are lucky
or unlucky?

Would you ...

Place more value on
truth or beauty?

Give more attention to
truth or beauty?

Expect to get farther in the modern world
with talent or with intelligence?

Would you . . .

Sooner bequeath to your
child talent or a high IQ?

Prefer to possess great
physical strength or
be naturally graceful?

Would you . . .

Contend that the
male body comes
closest to perfection,
or the female body?

Would you . . .

Say that sloth
or greed is the
worse vice?

Rather have more
time for napping or
for making money?

Say that someone who had nothing but leisure time should "get a life"?

Would you . . .

Judge a person who had nothing but leisure time differently depending on whether they used it for napping, watching TV, reading, listening to music, cooking, gardening, or jogging?

Declare that greed
is necessary for
motivation?

Would you . . . .

Think less of someone
who worked overtime
for the money, or of
someone who worked
overtime because they
love what they do?

Rather grow up rich
or be self-made?

Would you...

Judge someone born with a silver
spoon in their mouth differently
from a self-made person?

Would you ...

Say you value the struggle for
success more than the results?

Be more inclined to share
hard-earned wealth or an
unexpected windfall?

Would you ...

Say that you are a net contributor to the world, or a net taker?

Rather sit next to the founder of a business or the founder of a charity at a dinner party?

Be more impressed by someone who had amassed great power or by someone who had accumulated great wealth?

Would you . . .

Prefer to have more money or more power at work?

Tend to buy something for
its quality or for its label?

Would you . . .

Tell someone
what you spent
on something
you bought?

Would you . . .

Say that you've ever been attracted to someone, even platonically, due to their wealth?

Suspect the motives of someone who married far above their economic status?

Would you ...

Rather outlive
your money or
have it outlive
you?

Compromise your lifestyle
in order to leave more
money to your children?

Put your parents in a
nursing home against
their will?

Take on the financial
burden of caring for
your parents in their
old age?

Would you . . .

Automatically divide your estate equally among all your children?

Would you...

Sue your sibling if your parents left them the whole inheritance?

Would you ...

Be able to hierarchically order without hesitation your duty to your spouse, employer, children, parents, country, friends, and conscience?

Contend that you attend to the above in that order?

Would you...

Ever resent a friend's happiness?

Feel guilty for being truly content?

Loan your sibling a lot of money?

Would you . . .

Charge them interest?

Take a job working
side by side with
your spouse?

Would you . . .

Fire your spouse if necessary?

Would you . . .

Say that you live
more for yourself
or for others?

Contend that you live more in the past,
the present, or the future?

Would you . . .

Rather lead or follow?

Be a better teacher or student?

Consider the definition
of evil to be subjective?

Would you . . .

Contend that evil is necessary in the world?

Give the mother the final word in matters of child rearing?

Would you...

Give the final say regarding circumcision to the mother or to the father?

Would you . . .

Rather keep
your teeth or
your hair?

Rather have your
spouse keep their teeth
or their hair?

Would you...

Give up your career
for another person?

Have more respect for someone who
gave up their career for love, or
someone who gave up love for a career?

Confess to your mate after
having a one-night stand?

Would you . . .

Want to know if your lover
had a one-night stand?

Adopt a baby of
another race?

Place adoptive
children only
with parents of
their own race?

Would you . . .

Would you ...

Say that you look better dressed or naked?

Expect your partner to say that you look better dressed or naked?

Would you ...

Claim to be comfortable with nudity
in culture?

Take your family to a
nude beach?

Say that you like
yourself better than
you like other people?

Would you . . .

Say that you like yourself better than
other people do?

Sacrifice two years at the end of your life
to gain one year now?

Would you...

Sacrifice a year's salary to fix your
worst physical feature?

Would you . . .

Accept a fatter
spouse in order to be
thinner yourself?

Accept a 50 percent
impotence rate in
order to keep all of
your hair?

Would you ...

Expect to go farther in life with or without a spouse and family?

Befriend people just because they could help you get places?

Feel obliged to inform your parents, before introducing them to your new love interest, that he or she was of a different race or religion?

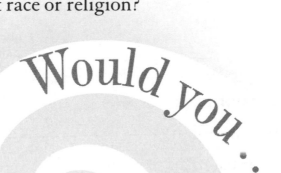

Would you . . .

Find it more difficult to admit to alcoholism, drug abuse, impotence, or bankruptcy?

Give up your place in a
life raft to a woman,
child, or elderly person?

Give up your place at
the top of an organ
transplant list to a
woman or child with
the same condition?

Would you . . .

Would you . . .

Encourage your child to tell on a classmate who was cheating?

Return an item inadvertently added to your shopping bag?

Would you ...

Hire someone who was clearly smarter than you?

Rather befriend people smarter than you, dumber than you, or intellectually equal to you?

Sleep your way to the top?

Would you . . .

Use your position to gain sexual favors?

Have your spouse followed to find out
whether they were cheating on you?

Would you...

Search your child's room without
their knowledge?

Would you ...

Have married your spouse if they had been penniless and likely to remain so?

Advise a friend against marrying someone very poor?

Would you . . .

Assist your spouse in a suicide?

Want your spouse to seek
sexual satisfaction elsewhere
if you were permanently
incapacitated?

Live within twenty miles of a nuclear reactor?

Would you . . .

Work in a nuclear power
plant on a daily basis?

Want fashion models to be the weight, size, and build of the average American?

Be more apt to make a purchase from a persuasive salesperson who was attractive than from one who was not?

Would you . . .

Would you . . .

Live in a house where a murder had once taken place?

Move into a house if the previous owner had committed suicide there?

Would you . . .

Wonder about a person who
decided never to have a family?

Have a child if you knew
beforehand that their life
would be short?

Prefer to be more in
love with your spouse,
or to have them be
more in love with you?

Would you . . .

Marry someone you loved, knowing that
they loved someone else more than you?

Physically strike your spouse for any reason?

Would you...

Leave your lover immediately if they struck you?

Would you . . .

Fight harder for a person's right to say whatever they liked, or for another person's right to be protected from racism or bigotry?

Defend a person's right to deny the Holocaust?

Would you . . .

Attend the execution of a
person sentenced to death?

Ever consider the death
penalty an appropriate
punishment for a person
under the age of eighteen?

Expect a raise every year, even if the company you worked for did not make more of a profit every year?

Would you . . .

Expect a larger raise in those years when your company made larger profits?

Agree to have dinner with
a stranger you met in an
Internet chat room?

Would you . . .

Hire an escort to
accompany you to an
important event if
you could not round up
a date?

Would you ...

Demand an
engagement ring
back if you broke
off the engagement?

Accept an engagement ring from
your boyfriend, knowing he had used
it in a previous, rejected proposal?

Would you . . .

Prefer the United States to use nuclear weapons to ensure a military victory, or to take the chance of losing in conventional warfare?

Sell United States military secrets to another country for cash if you knew that you would never get caught?

Consider nuclear warfare
or chemical warfare
more inhumane?

Would you...

Rather have to defend yourself against a
nuclear attack or a chemical warfare attack?

Seek to retrieve land stolen from your ancestors at any time or place?

Would you...

Give up land you owned as compensation to Native Americans if it had been stolen in the United States expansion?

Would you . . .

Seek a manslaughter conviction for someone who had run a red light and accidentally killed one of your loved ones?

Seek to prosecute a police officer for accidentally shooting and killing an unarmed person?

Would you...

Choose to be reincarnated or
to go directly to heaven?

Prefer to find out that there is no
heaven or hell, or that there is?

Claim that overall, men should behave more like women, or women more like men?

Would you . . .

Prefer to work only with women or only with men?

Sleep with a friend's mate?

Would you . . .

Confront a friend who was flirting with your mate?

Would you...

Prefer to do one thing in life very well, or many things adequately?

Prefer a life that follows a basic plan or one full of surprises?

Would you ...

Be more reluctant to become involved with someone because of differences in culture, race, wealth, age, values, or political beliefs?

Say that a good relationship depends more on common interests or on passion?

Pay ransom to kidnappers without going to the police?

Would you . . .

Blackmail someone to protect your own interests?

Wear decidedly unfashionable clothes in public?

Let someone's attire influence in any way your impression of them?

Would you . . .

Boycott a store that discriminated against some races or sexual orientations?

Quit your job in a company that discriminated against some races or sexual orientations?

Would you...

Expect the biggest strain on your relationship to be caused by infidelity, by boredom, or by money problems?

Be angrier to discover that your spouse had had an affair or had spent your life savings?

About the Authors

EVELYN MCFARLANE was born in Brooklyn and grew up in San Diego. She received a degree in architecture from Cornell University and has worked in New York and Boston as an architect. She now lives in Florence, Italy. In addition to writing, she paints and lectures on architecture for the Elderhostel programs in Florence.

JAMES SAYWELL was born in Canada and lived in Asia as a child. Besides questions, he designs buildings and furniture. He divides his time among the United States, Italy, and Hong Kong.